Nono's Kisses

for Sephardic Children

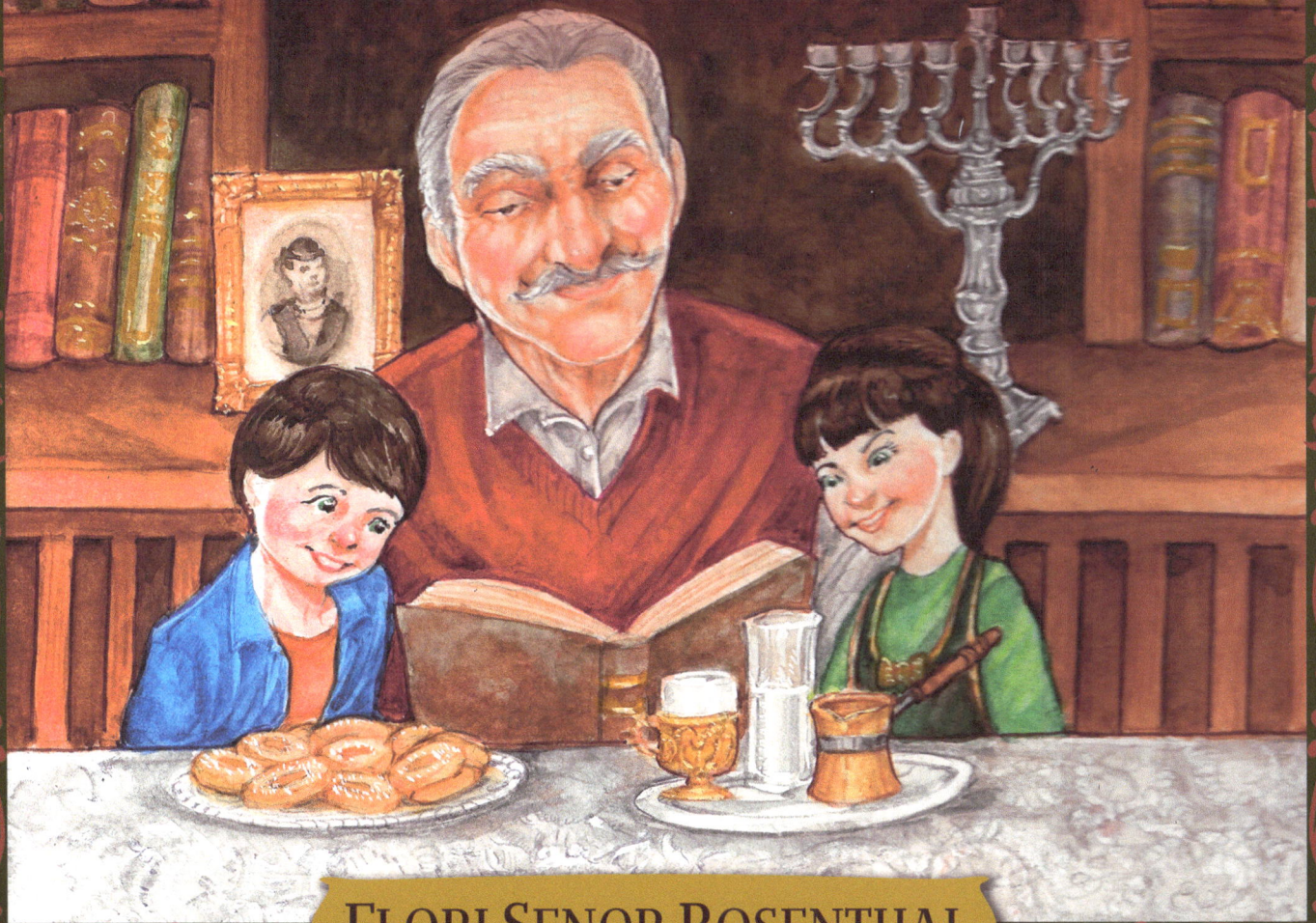

FLORI SENOR ROSENTHAL

The intent of this book is to offer information of a general nature to help the reader attain insight of a general nature on the language being written within the contents.

Published by Legacy and Literacy Scholastic Media

www.NonosKisses.com

Printed in the United States of America.

Book Cover Design by Kathi Dunn

Illustrations by Flori Senor Rosenthal and Graphic Artist Steve Ferchaud

Library of Congress Cataloging-in-Publication Data

Rosenthal, Flori Senor.

Nono's Kisses for Sephardic Children

Flori Senor Rosenthal --- 1st Edition

ISBN-13: 978-0692221686

Legacy and Literacy Scholastic Media

ISBN-10: 0692221689

Library of Congress Control Number: 2014913400

LEGACY AND LITERACY
Scholastic Media

Los Angeles ❧ Madrid ❧ Jerusalem

I lovingly dedicate this work to my parents,
Beatrice and Gabriel Senor, of blessed memory.
You kindled my passion for all things Sephardic, our heritage and our culture.

To my husband, Michael - You have enriched my traditions by melding them with yours.

To our children, Bianca, Geoffrey and his wife Heather, Erica and her husband Elliot
and our grandchildren, Jacob and Chloe -
You have given us the opportunity to continue where your grandparents left off.

L'dor Va'dor
From Generation to Generation

Acknowledgments

To my father, Gabriel Senor, of blessed memory… Thank you for teaching me to love the rich traditions of our Sephardic heritage. When I was a child you would recite to me Ladino phrases, many of which made me laugh. It was you who inspired me to write and illustrate this book. I thank you for all your love.

To my mother, Beatrice Auslander Senor, of blessed memory… Because of you I appreciate my Ashkenazi heritage. But what a surprise it was to all of us, to find out, that you too, were Sephardic! Thank you for being my mother and for all your love. No ay amiga en el mundo mas ke la madre.

To my husband, Mike…Thank you for loving me and supporting me during our journey through life. I loved sharing with you my ideas for various illustrations and getting your feedback. It meant a lot to me because it showed that you cared about my dream. Thank you also for making me laugh when laughter was the best medicine.

To my daughter Bianca, my mini me… When you were very little for days you would wake up and take out every towel we had in the linen closet. You would then line up the towels in rows and gently place every doll and stuffed animal you had on each towel. You were too little to tell me why you were doing it but it seemed important to you. So despite the added laundry and mess I had to clean, I let you do it. Thank you for inspiring me to share those precious moments with you in this book. I am so blessed to be your mother and so proud of the wonderful and caring person you are. Atyo!

To my son Geoffrey, my sunny boy… You could be a little mischievous when you were a little tyke. One day I bought some shortbread cookies that I shared with the three of you. You liked them so much that when I was not looking you ate the rest of the package all by yourself. While you did not get a stomach ache, the cookies were so rich, that you said you would never eat shortbread again. And you never did! Thank you for keeping me alert and making me laugh. I feel very proud that you are an awesome father and very blessed to have you for a son. El ojo ve, el korason dezea!

To my daughter Erica… You were everyone's kukla and everyone did call you kukla. You were always smiling and happy but no one could ever hold your hands. We used to laugh about it and say that you would probably grow up to be a pianist or surgeon. Well you did learn to play the piano, the violin, the base, and the guitar! Thank you for keeping me entertained with all your passions. I am blessed to have such a talented daughter and am very proud of all your accomplishments. En kada dedo un marafet!

To my dear family friend, Lauren Winkler… May your memory be a blessing. You were not here for very long but you touched the lives of many across the world. Your giving heart and work with *To Save a Child's Heart Foundation*, is an inspiration for many. Thank you for the lessons you taught me. Tener mano avyerta!

To my Tia Evelyn and Uncle Harry... Thank you for always being there for me when I needed to talk to someone. Thank you for your special wishes for me. I love you both so much. Munchos i buenos!

To my dear friend, Luisa, of Luisa Chocolatiere… You keep me sane with your fabulous, hand-made, chocolates, the best in the world! If it was not for you, I would not have met Stella Togo and would not have finally carried out my dream of writing my book. Thank you for being the wonderful friend you are.

To Stella Togo… In life, if we are lucky enough to see them, we are given opportunities to help us enable our dreams. Mine came in the form of a person, Stella Togo, who encouraged me to write my book, now. Thank you for giving me the confidence and the help I needed to get started writing and illustrating this book.

To my team of incredible professionals, Steve Ferchaud, Kathi Dunn, Jake Greenberg and my design team at CreateSpace… Thank you for your expertise and talents that brought my illustrations and concepts to life. You all amaze me!

To my cousins, Gloria and Elliot Gorlin… You are two very talented people! Thank you for your love and for always being there to help me out with your expertise. I love you!

To Rachel Amado Bortnick, an incredible person... You are the heart and soul of the Ladino language and you are my inspiration. Thank you so much for all the time you spent correcting my Ladino and helping me to get it perfect. I feel truly blessed that you took the time to help a stranger with her dream. I look forward to learning more from you and to one day having a conversation with you in person and in Ladino!

To Rabbi Mendy and Kreinie Paltiel… Thank you for your encouragement and cultural assistance. I feel truly blessed to have you in my life.

To my extended family and friends, old and new and too many to list. YOU know who you are! Thank you for all the love and support you have given me throughout my life's journey. I am a better person for having you in my life. I love you all very much.

To my generations past, you who came before me… You are the whispers in my ears that I will always feel in my heart. While I may have never met you, it is from you I am blessed.

A Special Note From Flori

I come from a "marriage", actually a family of mixed cultures-or so I thought. For most of my life I knew my father was a Sephardic Jew and my mother an Ashkenazi Jew. I was therefore blessed with learning about the customs and traditions of both cultures from each of my parents. I was also lucky that they could never talk in a "strange" language when they did not want me to know what they were talking about. However, there were always fights between my parents on which customs to follow. To my mother's dismay the Sephardic customs usually won out. But that turned out to be okay because after my children were born my mother was contacted by a long lost relative who told her, her father's family was actually Sephardic even though they had lived in Eastern Europe!

I always leaned more toward my Sephardic heritage. As a child, I loved going to the Sephardic Jewish Center in the Bronx with my father. I loved to hear the melodies of the prayers which sounded so exotic to me. One of my favorite things to do was to sit with the women in the balcony where I was the center of attention—and of course there was always the food. I still enjoy to this day— the borekas, roskas, and fijones, just to name a few. My father was a great cook of these Sephardic delicacies and taught me well.

I wanted so much to speak Ladino (also known as Judezmo) and be able to have a conversation with my great Tia Sarah who never spoke English. But no one seemed to have the time to teach me. So I learned Spanish in school and kind of knew how to pronounce some of the Ladino changes, but it was not the same. Since we did not live near my grandparents or other family I had no one to practice with anyway.

I often wondered about Ladino as it appeared to be a language in jeopardy or near extinction However, I always thought to revive it somehow. For 20 plus years I had the idea of writing and illustrating a children's book in Ladino but never made it a priority.

Nono's Kisses for Sephardic Children is a compilation of nine illustrations of nine phrases in Ladino, the language of Sephardic Jews. It is my hope that children, parents and grandparents get much more out of simply translated words. I believe that by adding an illustration to a proverb or phrase, it can lead to a conversation, using the beautiful Ladino language.

Engage your children with the words that you find associated with these illustrations. If the image gives you words for parts of the face, ask them to point to their own and name the parts. And when you are not reading the book, but perhaps driving in the car, ask them to find examples of the words that they learned from the book, for example, the colors of the cars that they see. Let the words tickle their tongues so that they love the language and the culture. The existence of our culture depends on how well we pass it down to our children. My goal is to make learning Ladino fun so they will embrace it and pass it down to their children.

A number of the illustrations are from actual events that I experienced with my children. So I hope that parents will discuss their experiences with their children that represent the same phrase. For example, "Atyo!" - What might have startled them or you in a funny way?

As a special treat and to have more fun with the book, special butterflies were created and can be found hidden somewhere in each of the illustrations. Let your children have fun looking for those butterflies.

Enjoy!

Flori Senor Rosenthal
www.NonosKisses.com
www.FloriSenorRosenthal.com

Pronunciation Chart

The following is the Ladino Alphabet (LAD), with its English pronunciations examples (EPE). We follow the spelling rules of Ladino as established by the publication Aki Yerushalayim (http://www. aki-yerushalayim.co.il/index.htm - once at this site click anywhere on the cover and it will lead you to a pronunciation graphic).

LAD	EPE	LAD	EPE
A/a	arm, father	M/m	man, mama
B/b	bad, lab	N/n	no, normal
CH/ch	chicken, catch	NY/ny	canyon, banyon
D/d	did, done	O/o	original, core
DJ/dj	jumbo, just	P/p	pet, map
E/e	bed, met	R/r	red, try
F/f	find, fox	S/s	sun, miss
G/g	give, flag	SH/sh	she, crash
H/h	heavy, hair	T/t	tea, getting
I/i	heat, see	U/u	blue, food
J/j	vision, pleasure	V/v	very, favor
K/k	cat, back	X/x	example, rags
KS/ks	ax, picks	Y/y	yes, yellow
L/l	land, lamp	Z/z	zoo, lazy

Please note the following special sounds:

DJ/dj   jumbo, just

J/j   vision, pleasure

Also remember that the vowels have only one sound each:

A is always pronounced as in AH

E is always pronounced as in BED

I is always pronounced as the "ee" in SEE

O is always pronounced as in OH

U is always pronounced as in PRUNE

On the following pages you will find a statement in English about each illustration. This will help you to start a conversation with your child about what you see. You will then see an expression in Ladino, with its English translation, which expresses what is going on in the picture. Then there's a question in Ladino, with its English translation. The words in the list are offered in both English and Ladino, to help your child answer the questions.

Please note that the syllable that should be stressed in Ladino is underlined.

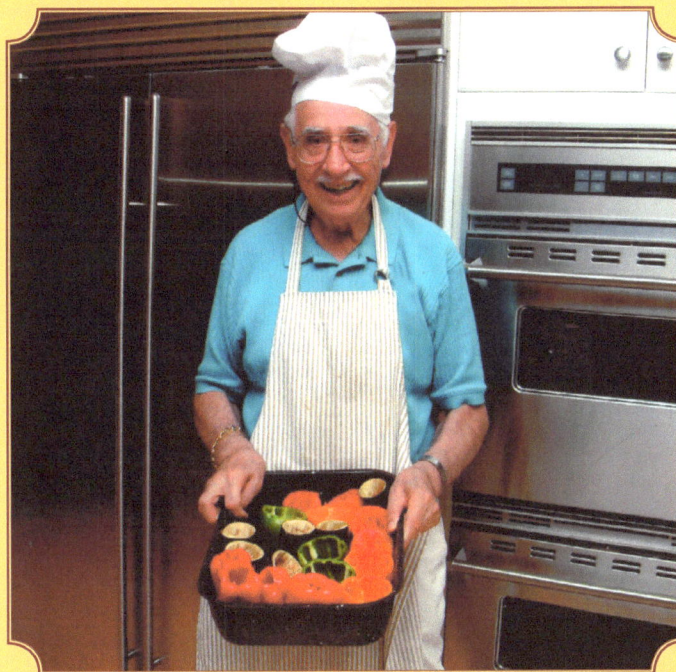

My father, Gabriel Senor, of blessed memory.
He loved to cook Sephardic dishes for his children and grandchildren.
Here he is as "Chef Nono" teaching us the steps to make
"Verduras Rellenas" (stuffed vegetables with meat and rice).

Look Who Is Sick Today!

A<u>ty</u>o!
Dear Lord!

Ken es<u>ta</u> ha<u>z</u>ino oy?
Who is sick today?

The baby = *El be<u>be</u>*
The horse = *El kava<u>y</u>o*
The cat = *El <u>ga</u>to*
The duck = *El <u>pa</u>to*
The bear = *El <u>l</u>onso*
The bunny = *El tau<u>shan</u>*
The doll = *La <u>kukl</u>a*

Look Who Is Dressed In Grandma's Clothes!

La kukla de la Nona!
The doll of Grandma!

Ke esta vistyendo?
What is she wearing?

The dress = *El fostan*
The skirt = *La fusta*
The shoes = *Los kalsados*
The hat = *La takya*
The purse = *La chanta*
The shirt = *La kamiza*
The fur coat = *La samarra*
The pearl necklace = *El yadran de perlas*

Look Who Is Having A Birthday!

Munchos i buenos!
May they be many and good!

Kuantos....
How many...

Balloons = _Balones?_
Presents = _Regalos?_
Girls = _Ijikas?_
Boys = _Ijikos?_

1 = _Uno_		11 = _Onze_
2 = _Dos_		12 = _Dodje_
3 = _Tres_		13 = _Tredje_
4 = _Kuatro_		14 = _Katorze_
5 = _Sinko_		15 = _Kinze_
6 = _Sesh_		16 = _Dizisej_
7 = _Syete_		17 = _Dizisyete_
8 = _Ocho_		18 = _Diziocho_
9 = _Mueve_		19 = _Dizimueve_
10 = _Diez_		20 = _Vente_

Look How Many Instruments She Plays!

En kada dedo, un marafet!
In every finger another talent! (A skillful person.)

Ke instrumento tanyes?
What do you play?

The guitar = *La gitara*
The piano = *El pyano*
The violin = *El violon*
The xylophone = *El zilofono*
The songs = *Los kantes*
The music = *La muzika*

Look Who Is Making A Donation!

Tener mano avyerta.
To have an open hand. (To be generous.)

Ke ves?
What do you see?

The window = *La ventana*
The curtain = *La kortina*
The tablecloth = *El mantel*
The table = *La meza*
The wall = *La pared*
The floor = *El kat*
The ball = *El top*
The toys = *Los djugetes*
The good deed = *El zehut*
The charity box = *La kashika de sedaka*
The coin = *La para*
The street = *La kaye*
The building = *El edifizyo/La fragua*

Look What The Boy Wants To Eat!

El ojo ve, el korason dezea.
The eye sees, the heart desires.

El ijiko va a komer...
The boy is going to eat...

The ice cream = *La dondurma*
The doughnuts = *Los birmuelos*
The candy = *El konfite*
The cake = *La torta*
The ring shaped cookies = *Las roskas*
The rice pudding = *El sotlach*
The stuffed pastry = *La borreka*
The baked almond cookies = *Los marunchinos*

Look Who Is Hanging Out With Mother!

No ay amiga en el mundo mas ke la madre.
There is no better friend in the world than your mother.

Ke ves?
What do you see?

The bed = *La kama*
The pillow = *El kavesal*
The pillowcase = La *fronya*
The blanket = La *manta*
The bed sheets = Las *savanas*
The mattress = La *kolc*ha
The book = El *liv*ro
The sister = La er*ma*na
The brother= El er*ma*no
The lamp = La *lam*pa

Look Who Is Talking Too Much!

Avlas Muncho!
You talk too much!

Ke kolor es....
What color is...

Blue = *Blu*
Brownish = *Brunacho*
Gold = *Oro*
Green = *Vedre*
Pink = *Roz*

Red = *Korolado*
Silver = *Plata*
Yellow = *Amariyo*
White = *Blanko*

Object:

The goose = *El baba*
The shovel = *La paleta*
The sky = *El sielo*
The sun = *El sol*
The sand = *La arena*

The swing = *La kuna*
The slide = *La arresvaladera*
The grass = *La yerva*
The dove = *La palomba*

Look What Landed On Her Nose!

Mirate tu nariz!
Look at your nose! (Look cross-eyed)

Ke ves?
What do you see?

The arm = *El braso*
The eyebrows = *Las pestanyas*
The foot = *El pye*
The leg = *La pyerna*
The nose = *La nariz*
The eye = *El ojo*
The hair = *El pelo*
The tooth = *El/La dyente*
The head = *La kavesa*
The face = *La kara*

We hope you enjoyed reading this book
and learning your first Ladino words.
What a wonderful accomplishment!

Follow us at
www.FloriSenorRosenthal.com or www.NonosKisses.com

www.ingramcontent.com/pod-product-compliance
Lightning Source LLC
LaVergne TN
LVHW072121070426
835511LV00002B/46